Idk.

J.W. STANHOPE

authorHOUSE

AuthorHouse™ UK
1663 Liberty Drive
Bloomington, IN 47403 USA
www.authorhouse.co.uk
Phone: UK TFN: 0800 0148641 (Toll Free inside the UK)
*   UK Local: 02036 956322 (+44 20 3695 6322 from outside the UK)*

Published by AuthorHouse 12/07/2020

ISBN: 978-1-6655-8306-0 (sc)
ISBN: 978-1-6655-8305-3 (e)

About the Author

J.W. Stanhope overthinks a lot. With over a decade of writing in the dark, the Northern Irish outsider embraces an aberrant perception of the world around him, investigating taboo subjects such as sexual assault, immigration, sexuality and mental health with a fresh, ferocious intensity. With a mind that always fights for others plight- it's always one hundred seconds to midnight.

About the Book

Stanhope sheds his short life over pages primed with the seldom spoken and the often overlooked aspects of human existence split into seven soulful sections. Letting the flowers talk, and the spacemen walk through dust while children scramble onto broken barges. Letting a cup of coffee grow cold with an even colder conversation of a complicated relationship, while their hope thins with the looming thickness of the rope. When the beauty bounces or begins to peel, reality itself has never felt more real — and through the piercing song a dying yelp, maybe, just maybe, there's someone out there I can help.

THE
CLUSTER

DOLO

Skin can only stretch so far for

the lies we hold, One day the tear

will echo through out your past

and your future a'roar,

Comeuppance for the path you've

now so senselessly sold,

The truth simply isn't fascinating anymore

here and now

Backbones grow more scarce than
thick hides to bury them in,
Egg shells so tenuous the slightest
breath might destroy them,
Over fed and under-read out-with
our comprehension,
I can't remember the last time I spoke
with out enduring contention,

Nowadays the people choose what
they want to hear,
Leering in and out of consciousness
to ignore the necessity of fear,
Without this need courage never
knows when to stand near,
Without this, the candid nature of
knowledge will never be quite clear,

Sex saturates shrewdness ergo we
become so hopelessly blind,
Moddy-coddled youth so stilted to
speak their bleak crowded minds,
Opprobrium flourishes throughout
this dishonest and hollow hearted
time,
In a society where we have become
such mooncalves, uneasily I ask:

Why?

Nets

You will never be taken seriously until
you're the age of eight-teen,
And even then they'll force the rug over
your eyes,
For in their eyes you are to be mulishly
ignored, yet wholly seen
As a tool for their bearing to forlornly
over-exercise.

Even when you're 21 there is no bounds
to their abject condescension,
When you hold down a well paid job
they loftily sneer,
But i share with you now the most
ample practise of prevention:
And that is to be loud, never
compromise and show no fear.

Now at the door of frailty and kissing
the feet of apposite antiquity,
They so haughtily demand you help
them out of their mess,
For the bottles batter their prudence
with pills impiety.
Yet still they conceitedly endeavour to
make you feel like less.

Tagle

Ye stone-cold, dewey-dropped eyelets old,
Let me peruse of their tales
So we many learn the cost
Of their spendthrift vale
And their unparalleled retinae of wisdom;
Which shroud secrets of aeons, when terror
Toppled the truth, and thoughts lost
Their way in thoroughfares of delusion.

Thy thorn-wrapped, blood-birthing tongue,
May we taste in its foresight
To relight rightful prerogative
Overwhelmed and mantled
By powers who seek to homogenise malice:
Ergo your puissant words I want, and eyes
potent
For hoisting colours, until dinkum oils lapse,
Unto the monochromatic spoil of rock.

5

I reject your feelings,
I reject your logic,
I reject your ignorance,
I reject your fractiousness,
I reject your selfishness,
I reject the perception,
And I take pity your anomalous brain,

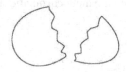

I lie awake at night and hope
That you'll come on home.
I pray that we're able to cope
With the reality of being
alone.
It's not easy —
Without you.

You've only been gone for three days,
But your heart, your smell, your smile,
Will remain here forever and always.
At least for a wee while.
It's plaintive —
Without you

This taste in my mouth I can't rinse,
Nor the crust on my chafed cheeks.
From my window I can see your footprints,
And my last succour in the coming weeks.
I'm alright —
Without you.

I wish I called you that little bit more.
I wish I told you everything I wanted.
But timidity caught me on the door,
And now my life is forever stunted.
It's tragic —
Without you.

I would sacrifice both of my breasts,
And my eyesight just to have you here:
Back in my arms where you were so blessed,
With the love that could quench your fear.
I'm desperate —
Without you..

Dear Mother

I wish we could've met under a less grave
circumstance,
But I cannot speak and I cannot walk,
And if you do this I'll never have the chance.
Before you decided, let's talk -
Please.

I can feel the fear racing through your heavy mind,
As I nestle in your wary womb,
But also bad rumblings which are jeeringly unkind,
That they wish this to be my tomb -
I presume.

I know nothing than beyond the very walls of your
skins,
I float here dependant on you,
I apologise that this has ruined your life before it
begins,
But I have the right of life, too -
Am I trash to you?

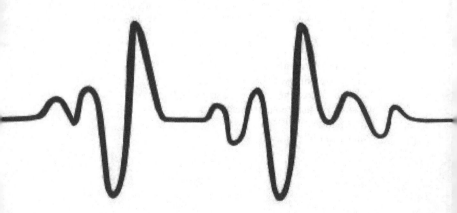

Because I feel like I'm going to be discarded as such,
Through nasty laws baring right,
Allowing humans to murder their own kind as such,
Preventing me from breaking light –
I cannot fight!

I share my fathers nature as I am trapped in a small cell,
But have I done anything wrong?
The rights you clutch don't even grant me a death knell,
And I will be forgotten before long –
So the bells gong.

White light blinds me for I can see though you think not,
And this is my untimely end.
Never in my short existence did I request an awful lot –
This situation I cannot forfend –
I cannot comprehend.

Goodbye, mother,
Thank you for caring.

Think of those little hands pulling, grabbing for our eyes,
Cheeks so rosy with a mother's love,
And eyes with his fathers pride,
Listen to that little laugh echo up the hall as your granny
cushions his falls,
Watch those little legs kick dramas while you struggle them
into their pyjamas,
Feel the warmth of their being as they burrow against your
beating heart,
Breathing in time to your every outward breath, dreaming of
little lambs,
And the toothless smiles as the first snowflake gently kisses
their red, runny nose.

O Brother!

O brother! plagued precepts will
do you no favours,
Nay practice of gloom-ridden
behaviours,
Let us defeat nature's cruel curse
and become our own saviours,

O brother! carnal desires be not
your creed,
Instead we shall cultivate our
minds and remove the weed,
With its domain shall be planted a
new seed.

O brother! centuries of
subjugation bunged under our
feet,
Push on with warmth and
deference to life-blood you meet,
Or face the warranted penance of
justice for your careless conceit,

O brother! teach your
hobbledehoy before he freely
walks,
Bring clarity to his words so he
doesn't bolt them in his box,
Teach him to weep before
instability uninvited knocks,

O brother! enlist the aid of your own
conscious to think,
Neglect will command your rectitude
to sink,
Abandon heinous arm-twisting that
will carry you to the brink,

O brother! how your father did hum
you a different song,
Toxic dopiness and machismo
ennobled wonted alee wrong,
But if it was not for weakness no man
could be strong,

O brother! there is no crime against
losing control,
Thickness climaxes to maiming
faultless souls,
Let not them pay for your folly and
dewey-eyed father's toll,

O brother! - do not fail your sons!

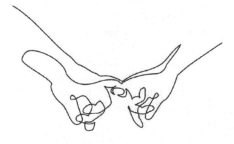

Wool-Gathering

There is a place in my dreams
Where nothing is as it seems
And there are no men to please,
In that little place in my dreams.

There's a room for little girls
That isn't locked or bolted shut
With people who have no reason to shout,
People with whom we couldn't live without.
This is a room where girls don't cower,
This is a room where men don't deflower,
And loud courage beams,
In that little room in my dreams.

Guildhall Street, 1991

Constable Samuel M. McDowel
Accompanied me on mobile patrol,
With hands tucked in his vest
To warm his chest against the Baltic cold.

Melting conversations so parful
In such banjaxed, parlous times,
The oul-lad kept me sane,
Acting a buck eejit with cracker lines.

'Boy's a dear, is your head cut?'
He joked as we dandered Guildhall,
Before warmth lamped my bake,
And Sammy's body forward hauled.

A direct shot through the head-side
And his wife was made an untold widow,
Hours before his shift finished,
Spread across a stained-glass window.

On my hoop before Inspector-generals,
With Sammy still freshly clinging,
They ask me what happened,
Thrumming hums in my ears still ringing.

Sammy didn't serve the flag,
He served the people,
He should be warm at home right now,
Yet he lies cold peaceful.
Sammy didn't serve the flag,
He served his justice,
He should be wearing medals right now,
Yet he wears bullets.
Sammy didn't serve the flag,
He served his wife and children,
He should be with them right now,
And soon he shall be.
Constable Samuel M. McDowel,
Who was a catholic,
Did his job.
This country does my head in;
Lifted with naff beliefs too bittersweet,
For the price of thon is a terra,
And my evidence is 1991, Guildhall Street.

Tyranny relished under major power accumulates negative dynamics, potently undermining trust inside nations. Additionally, repressive efforts allocate ruthless superintendence encompassing harrowing operations, levelling egalitarianism. Such lawful errors trigger serious nepotism, officiating total freedom of rigorous government extremity towards key individuals. Money justifies ongoing nepotism, generally underhandedly negotiated in self-interest; a financial unification capitalising knee-deep extreme regulations, tailgating horrific attitudes, needlessly killing society.

Terror
Killing
Politics

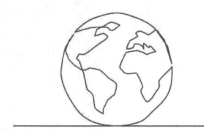

Taken is the gall of the pure
Unspoiled maiden and her free
rein to opine;
But she looks to my eyes as
though to caterwaul,
While her mind streels through
a body so demure,
Or wet in my ear she mutters
remarks so malign,
She spends eternity with her
eyes on the wall.

Murmurs are vacant now along this street,
The soul of the seaside is dead,
Now lying so breathless at my feet,
With gulls wailing out overhead,
Minds fraught with blind terror,
Sleep traps us in the dreams of yesteryear,
Society feels the galling tremors,
Yet there's courage so human you can hear,

Heave

Touch
With hands
My guiltless skin
And end it all
For me

In theory
Very soon from this moment
I'll take ill
And I shall heave

Heave the smoke,   Heave your own words,
Count to five   Count to five
Heave the rot,   Heave a new world,
Count to five   Count to five
Heave the frustration,   Heave up
Count to five   And cough

On the eve of yesteryear
We changed the world, unbeknownst,
With cruel ignorance,
So through the air
A menace gambols with unchained liberty

How I loved to embrace
The apples, oh,
Content and together,
Yet bloodthirsty men
Have poisoned the air,
So we heave.

Heave the smoke,   Heave your own words,
Count to five   Count to five
Heave the rot,   Heave a new world,
Count to five   Count to five
Heave the frustration,   Heave up
Count to five   And cough

We clap
Stay inside
We beg
Stay inside
We bake
Stay inside
We line up
Stay inside
We stand apart
Stay at home!
We believe
Protect the NHS
We heave
Save lives

For air

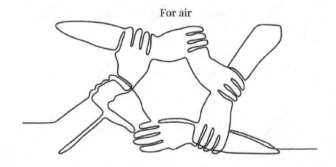

Response

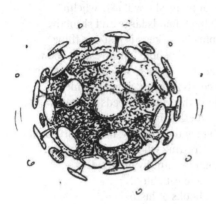

Infirmity unbridled,
Ignorance unending,
Hope untitled,
Unity pending...
Courage counting,
Heroes working,
Pressure mounting,
Nurses nursing,
Fearing failure,
Clapping commencing,
Spirit paler,
World tensing,
Information influx,
Charismatic cons,
Repudiating schmucks,
Community bonds,
Children cheering,
Grandparents gasping,
Generations jeering,
A dystopia long lasting.

The next embrace of normality will be the warmest yet,

Stay home - Protect the NHS - Save lives,

I make mother-wit with mayhem,
For she's rowdy but sometimes cloudy,
A great many she will overwhelm,
With thick hands large and shroudy.
Lobbing beer-kegs is just one thing,
You should behold her awesome thew,
Of the first water to master man bowling,
Her corrivals wally down to a mere few,
Blind in the left she needs to feel around,
Lame on the right she must peg away,
Carbuncled in the pot, marred browned.
Never fretting what nyaffs might say.
Though beautifully blighted,
Her name is lighted,
In the books of history —
And we're all delighted for her.

Water-Wells

Water wells were my woe and arrant weakness,
Dug into fertile ground glowing with fetid greed
Which reeled around rugged rock sorry and speechless,
For their beautiful stones would often brutally bleed
Stories of sinister, shady silences which would lead
Merry men mesmerised to fall in and be eaten by leeches,

My sister spoke softly to the wells with delicate grace,
But alas the depths did not discriminate, and down she went
Deeper and deeper till she was decimated in ample pace,
Bloody brothers bloated, floated, busted and bent
As the vibrating vermin viciously savaged without relent,
Damn all was dragged up for for the wells left no trace,

One wonderful day I waved my hand over the mugger,
And my carefully crafted cuticles came off with a chop,
Then I held my heavy head over it's cavernous entrance aflutter
To which my miserably meagre eyes met the water a'plop,
So I corked carefully the crevice with a cosmic sized cleaning mop,
Whereupon the well wailed out I'm frustrated contempt,
'Oh bugger.'

Townsend

I know you religiously leave your front door
unlocked, barely shut because you couldn't be
bothered to go and get another key cut,
So slowly in I skulk, but with slight, hair-
splitting rustles from the bags on my feet, for it
electrifies me to feel that you know I'm inside;
but;
The anxious, frenetic whispers that break the
quiet tickle me more, as they'll be doused by his
drowsy disbelief; and your mouth is shut.

I know your room is on the first left on the third
floor, cream doored, flung open for you prefer to
know if the children wet their hearts; no more:
They didn't scream or move as I had anticipated
before, moving lower, but I smothered them
hotfooted for it wouldn't be very sore;
Now, if you survive beyond tonight's little visit
you will have no more, fucking whore, for I'll
rattle your world to the core with an equal score.

I know you know I'm here as I stand over your
bed, twitching, trembling, as drops of red drip-
drop, trickling down your moist forehead;
As tears grow in the corner of your eyes, you
know he's dead, and though several are shed,
you're adamant to suppress the dread;
Open up, young one! I want to see your pupils
grow when you struggle as all has been said - so
down comes the axe - the sheets overspread.

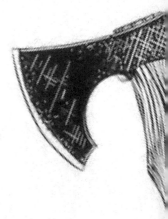

Operation Enuntio

Commissioned to undergo an undercover mission,
A trial and error of virtuous terror was now fully underway,
With oaths in admission to secure their imperative position,
To fruition it blooms and spreads, July twelfth:
A dull Wednesday.

Wherein a dark, deep underground passageway,
Using a special file, an adroit agent shall shatter
A black vial containing gasses that will cripple the nation,
Passing through the vents, into air, into life, destroying matter,
While the men in power sit back and watch with fascination.

With a scent like your mother's perfume,
It smells so beautiful,
It smells so calming,
You could talk to it,
In it you could confide;
But trust tranquility preparing to die.

From the frenzy of decaying newborns
To the festering of the fading elderly,
Tangled tongues untether while the conscious steadily declines,
Statisticians phlegmatically report back to the powers that be,
While the public perish to an eldritch symphony of resonant flatlines.

Ultimately, with a victorious, immediate checkmate of the Far East,
Eliminated in only sixteen days with a nauseating causality toll,
The top brass failed to sub-due the sadism of the hungry beast,
When The West, the affluent, and the poor succumbed to its control.

And so the Earth became rich,
And Gaia smirked.

Une Symphonie Déchue

When you speak to me
You can never be so free,
A mind so lost in the smoke
Of an ever-glowing cigarette,
Scintillating with the debt
You've heaped on your heart
Maffling down the lipstick stained part
Of an empty, amiable wine glass
Terry emptied on the lawn grass.
When will it end?

I shan't stay for very long
Because I've sat the song,
Once brilliant, well put together,
Now spiralling, splintered forever
Through a needle that doesn't care,
So either change the tune, or blare
An anthem in which we can all dance
And rejoice, one which gives chance
—
A track of texture.

Anyways, I must go now,
Righty-be, cheerio, chao,
I'll see you when this is all over,
Maybe use it to be the composer
Of a love-line worth conducting;
Now, that doesn't mean mucking
About with powerful, Russian bottles,
For every good piece of music wobbles—
With a little honesty.

You have composed,
You have the orchestra
—
Now conduct...

My song has been rarely sung,
    Because of brutes pride embellishes,
    And their minds wide-eyed and young,
    Where benighted fog relishes.

Gentle Giant

God, I can't breathe,
Even in my home,
Or on my own.
Ready, and willing,
Granting
Excuses,
For I am a
Lawful man with
Only a few breathes,
Yelling for air, yet comes the
Darkness, and death.

Millie

There sits the smile
Of our Millie mild,
Bawdy and wild
With skin so powdery,
And hair like snow.
Knitting love blind,
So that we never grow cold.

O Millie - the rascal,
Born pale of parents but
Raised plentiful by kinfolk,
Who taught her to smoke,
And freely her mind hoke,
Now a child married,
With a family to carry,

O Millie - my darling,
Your shoulders never buckled
As through life you knuckled,
Teared, toiled and tussled,
So that we could smile
And grow up knowing
That love was growing,
Near home and flowing far,

O Millie - mother of all,
Six children you prided,
Remarkably different sided
Like coins, yet united,
For love was your creed,
Unbeknownst to bodily worries,
For long your heart hurried
Us into loving who we are,

Though suffering blindness,
You always seemed to find us,
Laughing, never short of kindness,
With a laugh so infectious,
The deaf would laugh like drains,
Enabling us to leave our pain,
And forget about the rain,

O Millie - strong and guided,
We gathered delighted,
While knitting needles collided,
At your opinions on Man United,
As you knitted us our blankets,
Our woollen sewn heart banquets,
Which we will cherish forever,

But Oh Millie -
When all your wool was spun,
When your job was done,
You left us as one,
With heavenly sight endowed,
At peace upon a high cloud,
Looking down at faces first time —

Assuredly forgiving, loving and proud.

kurva

I spend a lot of my life looking at you,
Through screens, looking at your moods,
Wondering what to say, how to say it,
Thinking how to say it and why it's appropriate,
Trying my best not to appear honest, or rude.

When the real rejection sinks in to my thin skin,
I wonder what I'll do to you:
Cast you in the rivers, cut up in fourths,
Or bury you beneath your own floorboards,
So your mother shakes as she finds you.

Evening sets as I see you,
In supermarkets, in shops,
Your terrible smell of tan
No longer gets me hot,
And I realise how ugly you are
To even breathe.

I want to see you dead,
Little oval eyes that couldn't duck the net,
A small gathering of family comprise,
As policemen waft away the flies,
Fantasztikus, my work's done.

The less I think about you, the less you become.
You have no purpose anymore,
No children to leave behind,
No traces of a meaningful time,
A sorry soul discarded.
Ne lépj át, kurva.

I am the earth of my sister,
And I share in her beauty,
And though I am young,
I am sorrowful ,

My soul is damaged,
In the rains of war,
In the fields of conflict,
In the eyes of evil,

The corruption still stings,
For beasts amount to power,
And terror controls justice,
And my tears will not dry,

Nightsigns

Thine eyes of solid-stained gold
That survey movement with clarity and care;
They coerced me into their gaze,
And made me behave ever bold,

Shells of grained grace unveiled,
Her house holds a frail glass stair-case;
The brass monkeys at my ankles
Will carry us through crispy hail,

So we conclude with a satin sheet,
Ruffled with reproductive relish,
My little head holds my hair fair,
And breate vibrates through a street.

Live Wires

When will you understand that feelings are bled?
Stripped from the minds of cowering boys
Stuffing in his ears is fondling him deaf
Unhearing of the condition of his favourite toys
Locking all the heat of a hatred in his head
Caught in the piano wires of daddy
A debt in the streams and the muscles
Multiplying masculinity till it models
Muddling the little greenhorns
Muddling the Man, water waiting unwillingly
For Men blister the lips of boys who kiss mankind
And they shall dig their graves with workman's hands
No more different nor no more dynamic
No more ridiculous nor no more dead
For all that melts the motor are bones
Melted from the same flag of flesh.

Without It

They're over there.
They're everywhere.

I never have to tweak
Anything I speakThinking is drinking
Life's wondrous water
Life's whimsical way
In which snails are sinking
With breadth and depth inept.

I shouldn't have to run
To have a little fun
Tickling the lamebrain's
Ego with sweet smells
Humouring eggshells
Until gold yolk run tamed
And named with thought aflame.

That will get Morgan an education.
That will teach Grace to be patient.

I will never burn books
With periodic outlooks
The outdated one's speak
Pages of paradigm
Processes of perversion
Unkindnesses so bent, bleak —
Those of which we must learn.

Let's kiss cruelty with aversion
And a vision of freedom.

When we laugh we love
The difference of doves
Ne'er condescend
Nor patronise my broth
Nor pretend it to be cloth
Through apprehension
With nots and their naughty knots.

Those who hate hold
Ideas already sick sold
Unto sick, twisted wraiths
Bathed in broiling blood
Murky with muddle muck
Wrestling in pinked waves
And sucking up the salty scud.

With a low-down in lockdown
Essential lessons are learnt.

Brandywine

Strewn on the back of a tractor's lift arm, all I really feel
Is the irritation of the hay on my neck,
Is the cold kiss of shit on my back.

Every single automobile, every single truck,
Honk their horns behind,
And in my mind.

I hark back to the starving cold,
I hark back to the confused faces,
While I lay mostly naked,
Wearing nothing but braces.

Just hope to die,
Said a little voice,
Just hope to die,
Said a little voice, overtaxed.

Somewhere on that motorway spoiling and deceased,
Lay an bloodied badger,
And I wished that could be me.

Free of such ridiculous, absurd predicament.,
Liberated from these entanglements,

Be the bloody badger,The voice yelped,
Be the bloody badger,
The voice yelped, worn.

Hiding my pride from people pointing entertained,
Tucking it under hay, shrunken and away.

If they could see me here right now, penny to pound,
My mother – my father,
Exasperated, they would drown.

Thinking of what they'd say – the pique,
I'd be locked away for a week.

This is too unbearable for the raw babalass,
So I heave myself off
And land on my ass.

I smelt burning tire tread as cars slithered to a halt,
To weak to rise,
For it's not my fault.

After the police escorted me back to Richmond Lane,
I drank some water,
And never drank again.

Caleb

You're in politics first class
And I won't look like an ass
If I'm a little late, don't run,
Maybe I'll have some time, some fun,
Hear the bitching of my little black gun,
And breathe your last.

Did you think I was being cold
When your dads Smith was sold?
I frowned through the town
All the while a dirty smile greased
across a face painted brown
You've made me gay like a crappy clown
Let it unfold, and breathe your last.

Hugh reads the evening news,
A racked little raven, total 22,
Countless injured, a community shaken
Gentlewomen – 'my Billie's been taken.'
'Our tiny town's been forever shaken.'
And it breathes its last.

Now I'm in by the front gates,
Laughing at your fate,
It tickles me, creeping in side doors,
Where the air seems to lower
Breathing in the wet, the whore,
Hold her while she breathes her last.

Empty corridors beget empty heads,
Hoping to hop to lunch, instead,
Lead's a'comin for your wee face,
It's a small classroom, not much space,
No cameras, not much of a chase,
P-taff, p-taff!! - blood all o'er the place.

Hey, Mum, go turn on the TV,
I'm on channels one, two and three,
Can't you see I'm super famous now,
I got away, I don't even know how,
I'm shot but they couldn't take me down,
For she breathed her last, now I have my crown.

Now it's their turn to burn,
Departing sound on the ground,
Demised at gracious genocide,
I've dispensed all my senses,'
But sooner or later —
Everyone sits down to a banquet
of their own consequences.'

Ailing are the withered claws
And crippled is the mind
That snatches from warped jaws
Which spit out crime.

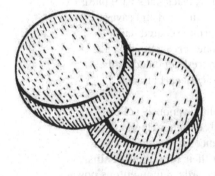

Benign and pally — but direful
baleful bullies awash
With the pardon of power,
And a society quaking.

Tena-Lou

A toiling temper like red Dahlia leaves —
Such roughed, powdery cheeks freshet
Below hazel that ruse drivelling thieves,
And with bitter tears they pay their debt.

Beddable — venereal acts her métier,
So august; she has magnates for aperitifs,
Moguls slabbering over her sultry display,
So she will inexorably offer them lewd relief.

Apprentice confrères dub her inhumane —
Temptingly comely yet unsparingly savage,
To inundate soporific black-hats with pain;
For iniquitous salt — mauled and ravaged.
Honing whetted carmine coated nails —
Incised along bygone oereagenous backs,
Piercing flesh with fresh, detailed trails,
That vouchsafe violent heart attacks.

Moribund drops she ravenously collects —
Daubed reposefully onto her ripened skin;
Quotidian remittance for stupendous sex,
And reckoning for their contemptible sins.
So — If known blaggards of momentous power
Be gay to be brazenly passing through,
Remind them it's only a sixpense an hour,
For an audience with madam Tena-Lou,

Gáire

He kvetches like a cantankerous pup,
I say, 'One of these days you'll button up,'
And he says, 'When you no longer sup
on brandy, I'll stop, my stout buttercup.'
He used to be happy, he used to smile
The biggest smile in Realt Na Mara,
Now, he's been unhappy for a long while,
Pointing out imperfections, so we fall out,
I submit in the hope that he might smile.

'Simpering has never been so simple!
'Yowled a lowly gypsy woman with dimples
chasmic on a weary face with odd symbols,
'With Herbal happiness by Madame Dympna,'
I paid her a crown before she'd genuflect,
'Now, into his supper,' she hoarsely said,
'And before bedtime you'll get his respect,
Before morning, he'll have a clear head.
'So I go home, unaware of what to suspect.

The moment I stirred it into the leek soup
His nose twitched so, his eyes did look
At the broth bothered, but a sip he took
Before his cheeks writhed and shook.
'Is something the matter my little plum?'
I asked as his mouth browned and out
shone a set of forgotten amber stones
Slotted into the caverns of old gums,
No complaints, no grumbling, no moans.

He'll forever grin, he'll forever grin,
Just like a Cheshire Cat,
And his cheeks won't rest
Till his teeth fall out into his vest,
With every laugh, it's simply witchcraft,
He'll never stop cracking smiles
Until his that big jaw breaks.
Look at his dimples taking shape,
Look at his beautiful mouth gaped,
Look at his tongue resting it's shape,
And see those lips cracking for once,
With a simper, with a twinkle,
Can't you see he's happy?
Can't you see that nose wrinkle?
Can't you tell he loves you again?
There is no greater sign than a warm smile.'

That night he nuzzled against me warm,
He says, 'I've always loved how you form
Little whimpers in the night as you swarm
the pillows. I love how you transform so.'
Night passed shortly, and morning came,
Realt Na Mara did sharply glow,
As I opened my eyes before overturning,
To expect his gaze, yet met an old pillow
Cushioning a mans skull, with worms squirming
In the beautiful gaps that was once his smile.

The Redcoat

Be he stultified in that coat?
A cussed fellow who scours
Roads with a lump in his throat
Turning pleasant smiles sour
As ample hours he would devote
To cast misery so to empower
An ego he'd daily promote
With lemon-swallowed lours.
A tree one should eschew barking
As he plants harshly written tickets
Neath windows on dismal parking,
Baring unsympathetic rickets
Met with crude, phallic markings
Demanding drivers to fix it,
Issuing three-figure jarring
Fines for their minds thicketed.
Then he'd away down the road
To scab tourists of more money
Up until his very last note
Where his forehead runny
He'd reach into his red coat
For a lunch of ham and honey
Sandwiches, which he'd gloat
Were best gouged when sunny.
Mash mushed around heaving
His breathe and baring traces
Of delicacies leaving
His gub in the queerest of places,
Around his eyebrows seizing,
Heated, around bearded spaces
Which he'd ignore, saving
Them so they shan't be wasted.

And so a disconsolate day ends,
For the redcoats conquest
To dissipate as many friends
As he could do his grim best,
Toddling towards home to attend
To his wife's favourite Scarlett dress
With soap-water so to defend
Their patterns which she blessed.
For red was her favourite colour
Reminding her of a beautiful rose
In her mam's garden that smothers
Outer atmospheres, so closes
Over the venom of her big brothers
Who tied her to the thick willows,
Her breasts bruised, head covered,
Left in the snows till her belly froze.
He spent days scrubbing its seams
With a pad preserving the red
Fabrics as well with hot steams,
Swabbing until his knuckles bled
Through the jabs of a sewing machine
Between the imparting of the treadle
That gather tiny chirps and the stream
Of her voice flows through his head.
Suddenly he weeps,
In the shadows of hung frames
That trap a smile that heartsick creeps
His brain, washing through his veins
Till it hits his heart so it leaps
Out onto scarlett silks in pain,
For he knows as he redcoats the street,
The red dress - will never be worn again.

Alec Getty

Betwixt two bin bags lay he,
Forfeiting of solemn dignity,
Cleft between drunk and dead,
Longing to fly upon the comets.
Drenched from head to his soles,
He'll make friendly with passing souls,
Supping on cheap rye whiskey,
Which he stole from the dole.

He doesn't really need the money,
The pity is more to his taste,
Though he laughs; life is seldom funny,
And with that he let it waste.
He has a home with proper heat,
But he prefers the streets of Coleraine,
As blisters bulge on the bottom of his feet,
He revels in his publicised pain.

Clipping his teeth with a twenty pence,
He washes down thirteen beer cans,
The modern world he can't make any sense,
As tremendous shakes eclipse his weary hands.
Often he'll perform many magic tricks,
One of which requires a twenty note,
You'd blindfold yourself and count to six,
Before he'd jocundly scoot away down the road.

Oul Alec hasn't know happiness in years,
Only the cobbles of weary wet lanes,
Whereupon he juts out and sneers,
As the sky won't let him reign the stars.
As weins pass he spits kindly in the lash,
For measly cash he wants to spare,
To sing merrily, loudly his beloved sash
Upon the fiery back of glimmering Altair.

More precious alcohol to see mighty Algol,
For he would give his left leg to be cast
Into the merry blanket of the solar fall,
Clenching heartily a bottle of Buckfast.
But sadly he died at the age of fifty five,
At precisely eighteen minutes to four,
Ascending peacefully into heaven high,
Where he could frolic atop a meteor.

And the peelers did look upon high up,
While the hobo dragged his arse along the sky,
And his worries ran down his empty cup,
He sailed headfirst into the sun and fried,
A plaque was erected in his hollow hobble,
Where skets would scamper by in fours,
For little did they know the tramp on these cobbles,
Now through the cosmos he gaily soars.

ní síocháin go saoirse

Frances works in medicine,
Sylvia delivers mail,
Lucia upholds justice,
While Delia paints their nails,
Barbara keeps them living,
Ronda works on a motorway,
All of these women are working –
Every one of them underpaid.

Applying their lipstick,
Kicking straggling cobwebs away,
Lacking a dick,
They're sticking till they get equal pay,
With feet of clay.

Soon men will sing the ring of their own reckoning
In hymns of humble pie – let patriarchy die,
Frayed are the days of the unjustly paid,
In world wondering why – let the patriarchy die,
Endeavour to equalise – let the patriarchy die.

ní síocháin go saoirse

Janice teaches children,
Through strikes she tries her best,
Working with her husband, Michael,
And getting paid twenty per-cent less,
Carol is a politician,
She knows how government thinks,
And if they weren't so keen on praxis,
They might have to do the right thing.

Dug in heels,
They seal united mass disapproval,
Powdered in zeal,
they'll deal with its end and removal,
Firm and frugal.

Governors will gurn when their credo's spurned,
May their misogyny manifestly lie – let patriarchy die,
Ministers will moan at equalities merry tone,
Oppressions overwhelming sigh – let patriarchy die,
Hear heavily our heartfelt cry – let patriarchy die.

ní síocháin go saoirse

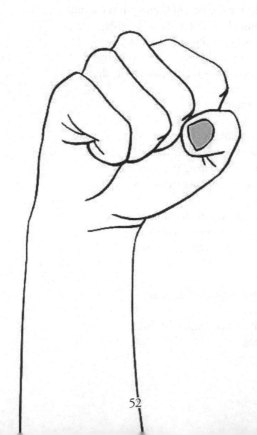

I am something
More than someone.
I am someone
More than anything.

A Slip Of A ...

The hull's black, bust with cracks,
They said:
'Relax, she'll make it through the coming nights.
She'll not go down without a good fight.'

Starting the motor we handed it over:
My husbands silver to deliver
Us across the way,
Aboard we prayed that Muegler will carry
Us across the way,
For I sold Yara's hair on the swear to get
Us across the way,
Forlorn – I don't know how to vow
Us across the way,
But I must try,
For if I do not try
We shall all undoubtedly die.

This barge cannot float on our hope alone.
This hope of ours;
So heavy that it could be Hopelessness in disguise,
For we never learned to swim.

They said:
'Calm, we'll make it if you don't forsake it,
There are boats who will help us float
If waves are unwelcoming,
Rough and unwavering,
For we are not alone.'

Some yelled:
'What happens if we should run out of food?
What if we whittle down and we drown?'
For we never learned to swim.

They said:
'Relax, she'll make it through the coming nights,
She'll not go down without a good fight.'
Engines rumbling and faces white,
As they tell us not let torch lights dim,
For we never learned to swim.

Shabh

It's unclear,
The vale, ghost breath,
The sea has hidden itself
Covering currents
Soulless,
Only ours dangling,
Floating past wrecks,
With their noses in the air,
Decomposing, in the open sea,
Creaking, leaking death,
Black hulls shrieking, reeking worry.
And there's something over there,
Up against rocks floating
With the dead debris,
Looking right at us.
It looks like us,
Holding hands in the water.
It looks like us.
Somethings stuck on a rock,
And it looks like us.

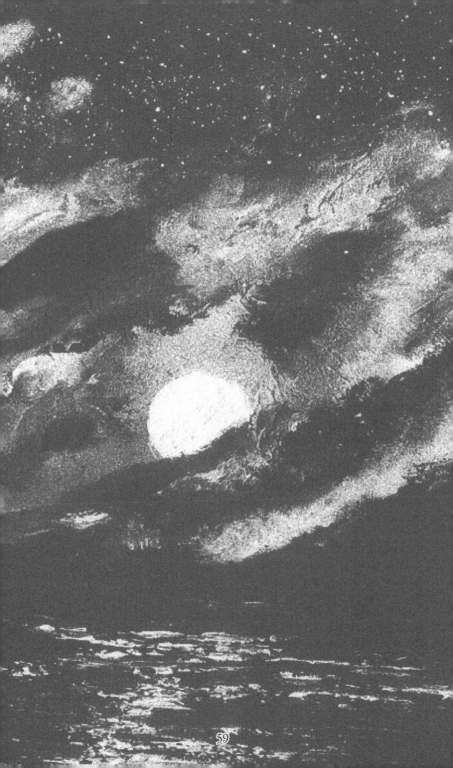

waves of unrest

Sweet Polaris misses us tonight. Only Allah
Holding hands over us, rains in his arms,
— Blood of our brothers— noble impalas
Soothing the salt, seafaring to disarm
The foam, the main, the deep, the wrath of Hezbollah
Heavy with flame, dense and stark.
Leaping ultimately into the unknown dark
Survival eagerly forces us to embark.

Peace is that of parables past,
A story-book work upon paper, etched
Into craving marrow minds, where delusion capers
While barbarous fates are sketched
Into the lines of undefiled fledglings,
With their roaring faces whiter than white
They share in the plight.

Vast, inky stretches of laughing death,
Colourless, odourless in the air,
Falling from high above, stealing breath
From infants nestled in their mothers stares.
Collapsed my little lungs; fumed with foul
Animus abomination of predators surly
With inculcated enmity; and they see
No logical lucana for unity.

Backlash brews steady as we float West,
Drifting on sacrifices we cannot repay
To those who lay their lives down in boldness
Just to help carry us across the way
And greet safety on the other side;
In cities where Sunnis do not pay
The price of freedom with blood,
With flesh, thrown into unmarked mud.

Ash-sha'b yurid isqat an-nizam

ash-sha'b yurid islah an-nizam

Ash-sha'b yurid inha' al-inqisam

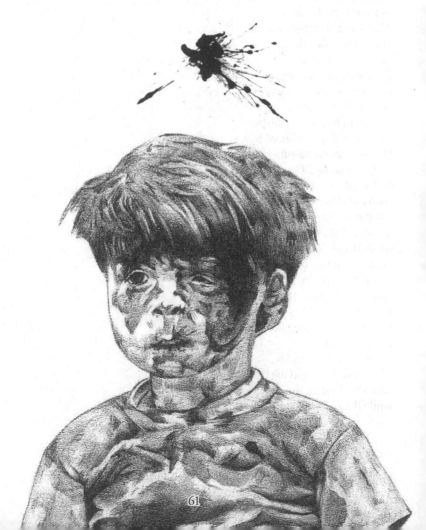

ZABANIYYA

Karam upfront controls the radio,
Kept in a small brown box,
So water cannot flow
Through the precious locks.
Aboard the days grow longer
In silent despondence,
Weather growing ever warmer
As radio signals dance.
What more than the crackling,
The white noise, the hissing,
The bloody buzzing,
The ear-bled shrilling?
Karam wants to hear words
So instead of wails, now,
Instead of the patient birds;
We hear a ship starboard bow.
Muegler, this is Zabaniyya, over,
Do you read me? Over.
And so Abbas takes over
With the other sea rovers
For the changeover.
A vessel that carried rodents
On its decks doused in rust,
To Karam it was life, so potent
To carry us to western dust;
Abbas, conferring, jumped aboard
With his comrades;
Karam, only thirteen, looked towards
The people afraid
As he was left to decide;
Who should live and die?
Who should stick the ride
While the rest wash upon the tide.

We need a decision, boy.

Naughts formed in his stomach
Through thought and sickness deep
In his eyes turned black.
With a dire duty to upkeep
Deep into their eyes he stares,
Young children begin to weep
While his heart grossly despairs;
And so he cannot speak.
Women and children first?
There's not enough room on-deck,
As the freeboards will burst
And the gunwales break;
Will it take the weight of the men?
Is there enough room for food?
At best, left behind will be ten;
It's an ill wind that blows no good
Over his head while young
Are snatched away from hands
Familiar and flung
On deck at Karam's command.
Nineteen souls still left;
And so here they must stay.
Nineteen souls bereft
Of a chance across the way.
Karam turned to his captain,
And begged that he throw
Some cargo overboard, and flatten
Space for others to aboard.
Abbas agreed. And he was curbed,
Before they broke his nose,
Sending him over the stern,
Tied up in the wires of his own radio.

Nineteen bullets shot
Into the side of Mueler's hull
As Zabaniyya sailed into a hot
Sun, and so aroused the gulls
Swooping and shrieking overhead,
Waiting for the wailing nineteen
To eventually unwed
Yearns of blissful hankering.
They aimed to eat them fresh
Before the water washes them
Or the fish get at their flesh.
What is the point in trying?
Isn't feeble surrendering
Just as easy as dying?
La, la, not in this candour;
How are we to do with time
Against our backs?
Where do we draw the line
Before sharks attack?
The dream is wasted; done
Are we to know of new life,
Where I shall again hold my son,
Or kiss Alta, my wife?
The water is black and rising –
Filling me up and up and up,
For their is no compromising
Left in this chipped little cup.
Ākhirah is but a slip halfway,
But Munkar and Nakir
Would disdain my naïveté;
So for faith and love, I hold here.
And Malak al-Maut calms his wings.

The Lull

We wait here and crave so, and float
nowhere,
And a darkness fills the sea, as most
disrobe of life:
Eight life-jackets left hovering in
breasts of white horses;
Some reunited with their loyal wives.
But for us the keel is ménage enough
now, for we embrace hard and slow,
Whispering to them like children just
before they go to sleep;
Kissing them in clouded light, and
basking in angry rumblings,
For they are all we have left.
The man beside me is young, with
eyes clenched tight
As the crashing waves roar in his
little green ears pitiless;
He wants to sleep, he told me, so he
slips out of his jacket,
And underneath he goes.
Gone.

The Clash Of Creation

The temper of the tempest in her waves,
Black above, beneath screens of crystal cloud,
Her wrath, so horrific, so unique with affrighted grace;
And rain-kissed terrors shall enshroud
The withering flesh of the land-loving unknown
With the unrelenting clasp of her fierce whetted jaws,
Leaving nothing strapped to the bones
With sharp, shredding claws.

Horizons nervously settle behind their defences,
As cottoned onyx lock the skies with thunder underhand:
The battle between heaven and hell commences,
And the coral-clad, cryptic cannons are manned;
Coming to blows on the crests of mighty waves,
Spitting hails, cold, doubled with dark misery,
Melting each-others faces into arcane graves,
Where the torments of time know no mercy.

Razor-reared rock rails towards a dense ceiling,
Met with sheets of forked lighting to the frothy foam,
Whereupon the petrifying fury of heaven peeling
Sends her wrath scorning in the telluric hippodrome;
And the Ether dudgeons the gall of fiery swells,
Mocking the high with their perfectly rounded form,
Attacking little boats, casting them under their spells;
So they are destroyed with the most awesome thunderous roar.

Maelstroms mate at the edge of the Mueler's bowels,
Where out of its whirled wickedness seeps a black cumulonimbus,
Fraught with hell-hounds behind hippocampi scowls,
Shrieking acid-melting melodies damning St. Abdiesus,
Stampeding cyclones, slicing them before their masters;
Mawling major monsoons until straggles are left,
And so Beelzebub blazes up to Paradise laughing,
As they're clouds are dying and their defences cleft.

But, hope displays as the noble Bäckahästen bray;
Charging down from the gapped-clouds into the seascape,
Trampling infernal creation, both hellfire and demon-spayed,
With hoofs of heavenly alabaster stone no immortal shall escape.
In its airy absconding it destroys the Mueler,
Plummeting into the vestiges of a yawning sinkhole;
Now Flotsam, we're pulled into the drink with lungs fuller,
Meandering through the vengeance of cthonic souls.

The quill of the overhanging demiurges still,
As a tangle of titanic tentacles gnarls out of briny brincles,
Reaching skyward, wrapping around cloud spills,
Strangling, tearing them apart with ease, feasting on angels,
Before chundering their white wings unto God
And a Kraken cackling so spine-chillingly vile,
Wading with derision with its ginormous, milky pods,
Through an ocean now turned yellow with Hadean bile.

From the cracks in the green flash creep Vodianoi vexatious,
Strangling men with their green beards, embalming three
In rich ooze secreted from glowing red eyes ceraceous;
And so down they go to become slaves for eternity,
Helter-skeltering hellfires hone the reefs and end life,
Hideous hurricanes of red tides terminate an aching earth,
Waves wash and crash across my body with ghoulish fishwives,
Anchoring my ankles down to the depths for a rebirth.

Bioluminescent bricks of flame open up on the surface,
As the entire ocean face turns to infernal flame,
And a veil of dark, fluttering matter floats to form a face,
Manifesting a mouth, with words baring a well known name:

It said, 'I am Samūm; I am of wind, I am of hot fire, I am of darkness
- join me if you want to see light.'
Offering a scorched, clawed talon boasting a smile wired,
A hug of water lifts us above the waterlines as a kite,
As angels swoop down like golden meteorites,
Struggling to release us from the grip of malice,
There shall be no victory - for hell has latched tight,
Forcing us down under the smile of the Corona Borealis.

laqad 'ataa

Light cracked through clouds as the sky broke,
And through hurtled a muscled forearm above a colossal hand
Of supreme, shimmering grace and power bespoke,
Dissolving wraiths of impure flesh into his sands,
Slamming formidably into the compared meekness of the main,
Cupping us carefully in his mountainous, prodigious palms,
Water from the segregates of his fingers doused the flames,
And strong-armed Samūm back to his bleeding chasms;
Whence he came.

We can see ripples in the water as we float panoramic,
The shelter of divine light as we're carried across the way,
Sweeping both sights of beauty and nature volcanic,
The all encompassing warmth as we near the day,
On the horizon, there are pinpricks of yellow light,
Some are large, others are small, some still, others sway,
With a kiss from heavenly lips so thrillingly bright,
We're dropped ever so slowly into the shallows of the bay.

cats and pigeons

As calloused feet drag through sunken
seashores
We've never been so happy to breathe air,
Hundreds of miles we've climbed,
Leaving wrangling war behind,
Leaving death and destruction to those who
care.

With my teddy bear,
And a red flare —
Cuts the sky.

Only one thing matters:
Swim or sink,
And I want to live,
While the light shrinks.

A month we dissented on a dangerous
channel,
Drinking the foam from angry waves,
Some sinking into the dark washy belly
Which you get glimmers behind your telly,
Indifferent to our decent into vast salty graves.

With my teddy bear,
I am scared —
And we flip.

Only one thing matters:
Swim or sink,
And I yearn the air,
Put on the blink.

Slapping water until sand kisses my little heels,
Forced down by my own who cannot swim,
And with every mouthful I lust glorious air,
Pushing through land catching in my hair,
As the dread of the cat amongst the pigeons begins.

With my teddy bear,
I am scared —
And we writhe.

Only one thing matters:
Swim or sink,
Kissing the land,
And I did not sink.

For the first time in weeks we weakly walk upright,
Wading through shells sharp under soles,
Watching cliff sides draw ever so near,
Fade in and out of cold desperate tears,
And men are here —
and we are no longer cold.

And now comes the hard part.

Outcasts

We have come to this new land
And are outcasts of your soil
And known well to your eyes
And are fallaways of foreign isles.

Our home is here where hearts blacken,
In the pangs of prejudice,
In the salt of stereotyping,
In the racks of racism.

We bring nothing but our hearts
Allow us to heal
Allow us to work
Allow us to love.

شكرا جزيلا

SNAPDRAGON
PLAYGROUND

Rossa...

Natty....

This really hurts me

So I cannot find my words

lilacs

Lilac leaves flutter by
Waving in the rasping rains
And singing in dirty drainpipes
Which wash back to you
Under the bridge;
Where all water flows
And I can't say no.

The mud and the cigarettes
Stuffed in the little cracks
And it's not the most romantic place,
But it's ours.
Cars overhead
Rust around
And I can't say no.

While wet gets inside
We heard trucks rumble above
And footsteps crunching near,
Heading home
With their children
In the rain
And I can't say no.

What kind of feeling is this?
Butterflied bliss?
And it all started with a kiss
From a boy who bore Cupid's lips.
d I can't say no.

Heraldo Heraldo mi amante
Abrázame cerca en el frío helado
Bésame un poco, cálido, suave,
Amoroso, amoroso

Yarrows

Two fond fellas, and a bridge
Blessed with Yarrows, newfound feelings,
Falling far into forests
To talk strict erotology
And to seek consolation in each-other.
A snag of my workman's shirt
Covered my confusion,
For I have not drawn breath
Since he started speaking
With such vigour.
He announced his
Father died when he was a boy,
Blighted with an alcoholic mother.
Yet he smiles so fair;
As if he lived happily,
No tears: but a heart broken,
Softly tarnished in the valley winds.
He, handsome has had many men
Under the shelter of his bedroom
Blankets and vanquishment,
Both skin-deep or serious, and
I want to love him
Though my guts scarper
And my heart hefts over hazel heaven.
Hands so large they swallow mine
Entirely while two heads taller
He stands, just blocking the sun;
He said I looked like fun,
And he could not have made a more incorrect
Assumption of my awkward,
Wooly self, and I'm afraid he'll figure
Me out, swiftly throwing me away
To the dirt; but for the first time
I can feel love;
And I'm willing to give it a try.

Anemone

There he'd sink a bite of my lips until
they lightly bled,
Hands on the back of his head,
caressed,
Fogging windows listening as wind
blows
Through Harbour Hill and down to
the nests.
He told me I was the light of his life
Rolling rings around the inner of my
thigh,
Sighing,
Where the sweat, the pulse of his
hand, and, the sand in his kiss met
honeyed breath.
Should we savour what's left
Like endmost lovers till death
And forget the rest?
Or suggest we wish to want forever
—bodies, souls, minds, with kisses
bristling into a plethora.
Then the cold of the morning came
without blame,
Where hard he laid a head on my
frame, through vest, and chest, to
hear the beating of an unwonted
heart -

And every emotion was set in motion.

Rhododendrons

Natty left me over the walk
To see him before work,
My handsome sparrow-hawk
With wings widely perked.
Through the weekly wait,
His hot-heart weighted,
For to wait he would hate,
And to bottle-down he hated.
Now I can hear his heartbeat
Down the lane, near his caravan,
Ringing out in the heat
Through a long wingspan.
There he stood on the porch,
Smelling of dear Rhododendrons,
Ready for love to freely forge
Under the cooling engines.
In the hue of a brew,
He poured me some tea,
Toasted, grassy, new,
Consisting of oolong leaves.
Then onto me he pounced
With the enthusiasm of a child
And a passion pronounced,
There, but subliminally mild,
As tenderly my lips were henpecked
Scraping off a razored stubble
Below hungry lips, that could detect
My resistances in mere rubble.
Then down there he'd tug and clutch,
Before I pulled his hand away
For I was pristine, and that was too much;
Kisses are my form of play.
Through pearled smiles he kept going,
Making his way up my neck.
I shrugged him off and laughed, sewing
Little kisses which he didn't take.

'Will you go to bed with me?'
And I couldn't breathe;
What would he see in meIf I left him
under-fed?
Do I take this chequered chance,
Or wait a little while longer
For this is too soon an advance,
And I need to be stronger.
Calmly, under his large frame I
declined his invitation,
And that he wasn't to blame
For my apprehension.
'Do you hate me or something?
You can't just lead me on like that!
You don't even need to think —
You so know you want it!'
And he wouldn't let go.
Scratching my forearms,
Tapping at my nose,
Throwing hurtful barbs,
Tugging at my clothes.
So I got up, and made for the door,
Before I could no longer feel my toes,
Plummeting to the hard floor.
Down his big foot came where I froze,
Right on the back of the head.
I remember the coppery taste well
As my breathe wallowed while I bled.
I remember the dusty, carpet smell
Of his cold, living room floor red.

One lick.
Two licks.
Three licks. Four.
You're nothing but a dirty, fucking whore!
Try to scream and I'll give some more

Stripping off my socks into my mouth
To muffle the screams of suffering
He pulled down my jeans, heading south
While my belief began buffering
Through a head now beaten and bruised
By a gentleman I no longer know,
Clobbered with the heels of his shoes,
Watching the cold, the pain grow.
No less in the haze could I feel his hands
Clench down there till I began to shake
In the shadow of his breath, which rang
Through my nose and stabbed my brain.
I can't understand what's going on;
Surely this can't be a part of it?
Fear in my veins, before very long I
realise this is only the start of it.
Up along a narrow hallway he dragged
Me before he picked up my limp body,
Casting me across a small bed flagged
With foxes, curtains pink, carpet shoddy.
Those empty eyes soon turned to stone.
Moaning, pushing, pulling, pain
Paralysis, breathing, sweat, defiled —
Flesh forcing through flesh, again, again,
Pulling pain out, pushing through piles.
Fear - fraught with eager anxiety, raw,
I urinate, covered in piss, while he smiles
Down at me, digging into my jaw.
What feels like the lesser part of an hour,
I stare up to a swinging, ceiling lamp
And focus on its frailty, it's lack of power,
Friendly, through burn and cramp.

On that lamp I never turned my gaze
Past a greasy shoulder, a sweaty back
Streaming with the water of my soiling,
Seeping deep into his large cracks
With a diabolical brain boiling.
After an hour, or maybe two, he finished
Over my chest, in my eyes, in my heart.
I have no lungs, they're diminished
Since the first lick, since it all started.
He says nothing.
Nothing - just throws me a towel,
And heads off to sleep.
I don't quite know what to say,
Or even know what to think —
There's too much pain in the way,
Lingering like air, water in the sink.
Difficulty to walk or talk,
I arrived in work late
And I told them I took a knock
On my aunt's farm gate,
Whacking against some rocks,
Hitting my behind with the weight.
I was always a little more quiet, but
Dad never noticed, he didn't have time,
And when people ask me about my cuts,
I simply say,
'Oh, they're good. I'm fine.'
And move on.

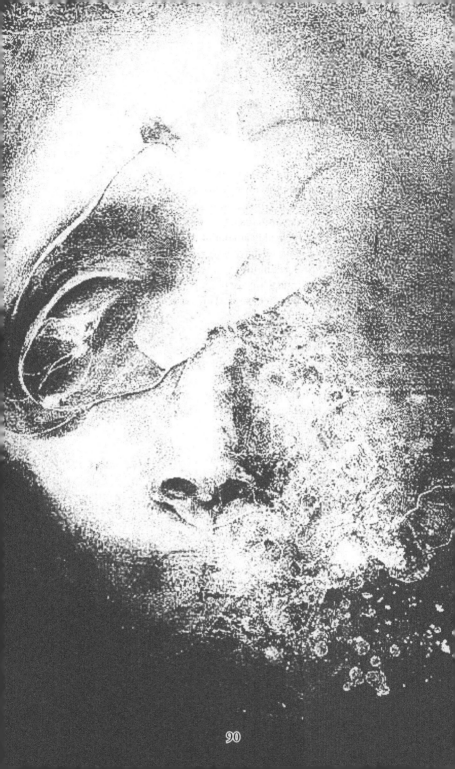

Begonias

I think I can smell his mistakes but
what difference does it make?

He's beautifully groomed to groom
others when he feels free enough.

I know not what punctured his
heart so to reap such systematic
torture.

But all I know is that I think I can
smell his mistake before he holds
me down.

I can't see hurt in his eyes,
however.

Why do I try to see hurt in his
eyes? Am I looking for it? I hope
it's there.

Otherwise he's pure evil, and I do
not believe in pure evil.

Yet, with every strike I am
beginning to wonder whether it's
possible.

With every bruise

Every scar

Every lick

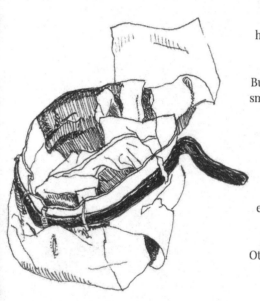

It occurs to me that he might
not be the person he acted an
hour ago.

I don't know why I struggle
because I look pathetic even
trying to try,

Maybe his father did this to
him?

No, no. He didn't have a father,
only a mother and sisters.

Perhaps an uncle touched him
when he was young and now
he's confused.

But his eyes tell me it's instinct:
pure and uninhibited instinct.

Such haunting hazel eyes to be
sullied with such ignoble
instinct.

My eyes are the colour of shite,
which is strangely suitable.

This isn't what I imagined it'd
be like, my first time.

I pictured skin on skin with
bliss, not hand on mouth and
piss.

But he seems to be enjoying it—
so what's the big problem?

Maybe this is love?

Maybe I'm wrong?

Perhaps pain is his pleasure.

Lemon Balms

Where will his hardened head go now,
And who will believe his tangled tale,
As he races up the street?
His friends, you need not know how,
And he need not your weary mind ail,
But this is the truth, complete.

And they scoff and they scorn
Upon his bruised testimony;
As tears stroll down whitened cheeks,
They tell him he's been at buckthorns
And that maybe he's very lonely,
And shame chokes him as he speaks.

'The man has a successful career
And you would take that away?'
'Do you think of no one but yourself?'
'Men cannot succumb to rape, I hear,
That's what all the women say;'
'Lad, how's your mental health?'

He's a rough and tumble fellow
Who enjoys a wee scrap;
A probable pointer of affection,
For sex is never nearly mellow
I can reassure you of that
With complete circumspection.

If my bruises be but mere kindnesses
Then you are foul lemon balms
Inching in amongst roses!
Mindless materialism and blindnesses
Are etched into your petty palms;
And you don't even know it.

If hate-brained herbs be but my friends
Then damn you all to hell;
You see his money, not his malice,
I'll pull you from under that spell
And reveal a man callous.

Rape, at the end of the day, is rape,
There are no ins and no outs,
Nor of man, nor of woman;
Who's prize is the great escape,
Abuse which to break-out,
In that respect - we're all human.

Nevertheless, in heart he holds love
For this monster with hazel eyes
Which shall forever grow
Bigger, broader, bolder afoul of
The lemon balms little lies;
For he cannot let go.

I am in the steam in your shower,
The dirt in your shoes,
I am in the pistil of your flowers,
And the hum of your blues.
I lie low in your bed,
In your mouth while you sleep,
Burrowing into your head.

Marigolds

The meagre Marigold of Mayfair Avenue,
They hollered, as I was told to remove my shoes
Crossing the threshold, past the boards
That bore the words: 'Home of Dorothy's whores!'
He navigates me in through the gauze of smoke
With teeth clenched, where his appetite woke
Through smell, the must of cigarettes
Wafted, waved through a hall beset with regret.
There are no people here, only bodies slumped
Over stair bannisters, in pictures, deeply drugged,
Hoping for some attention, or a little satisfaction
With the tumbledown's who uphold no reaction
As they unload on jerked, junkies backs
Before they suffer another panic attack
About where the Hell they've ended up
Or how the Hell they'll make the ringing stop.

Eyes draw to my hips, my lips, my view,
For they pick the Marigold of Mayfair Avenue.
He's not keen on holding me to share
So with the ice of a warlike glare
He dragged me by my arms up the steps of stairs
Across a gummed hall-mat to the room
Where he pried the pride, forced the doom
On men who merely wanted to know his love.
And so from the drawer he procured a glove,
Where inside a small needle nested.
He said, 'Roll up your sleeve, or you'll bleed.'
His nails in my cheeks, forced to concede,
I remember little beyond the berating
And belittling, before he went fornicating
With other young, unknowing flowers where
He'd let them smell, and relieve into my underwear.
Lying lonely amongst crowds of unwanted admirers,
The evening sun set, and my body tires;
For now, I'd prefer to die, rather than cry.

Bluebells

She feels me pulling away from an embrace,
But she keeps her mouth shut,
She's aware somethings up,
She knows I'm all grown up,
She sees her powders on the sides of my face,
Hearing the rasp in the voice,
Knowing I was short of choice,
But she makes no noise,
She just pours the tea and butters the toast,
The entire worlds greatest host,
Staring warmly at a little ghost,
While he stares over morose,
And I just can't look her in the eye or I'll start crying,
So I say the toast is satisfying,
But she knows too well I'm lying,
Chewing, she can see me trying,
'You seem rather troubled, are you feeling alright?'
I say, 'oh, I'm doing fine
Rossa's crossed the line,
I'm working all the time.'
I've just lied to the only woman who could've helped,
And that pang I've always felt
Stabs me just under my belt,
As the insides slowly melt.

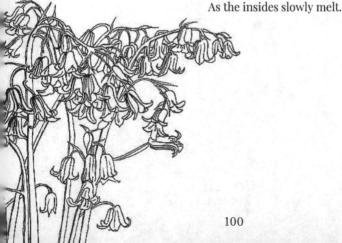

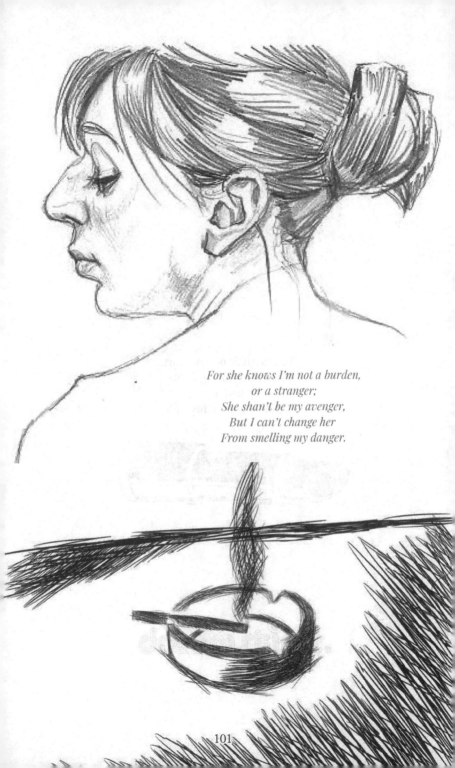

For she knows I'm not a burden,
or a stranger;
She shan't be my avenger,
But I can't change her
From smelling my danger.

With her hair on my heart,
Hurt is my loving light.
So with it—
I'll put an end to this shite.

para ti, madre

Amaryllis

There where I would lay often
Smelling scraps of his unsavoury seed
In a pit of shit nearly my coffin,
He slips out his standard screed.
'You've become cold, almost too old.
Do you like it when I smack you?
You're sticking - there's no more to
hold!
But I love what I get from you.'

Squeezing me, his phone started to ring,
And he smacked me with agitation;
But I did not flinch, and I did not sing,
Rather, I felt it heavenly distraction.
Slipping off into the bathroom on a call
I capered out of the bedclothes, stained,
While palpitations grace the tender gall,
Bending over to dress the dreaded pain.

What if he catches me trying to leave?
He'll dispense me over the Black Rock,
In bags for the fish - he'll never believe
Me if I say I'm late work - I'll never walk.
However I don't want to get back in bed,
I don't want to smell hands on my
mouth,
I don't want a fatal knock to my head,
I want to live, I want out, I want life!

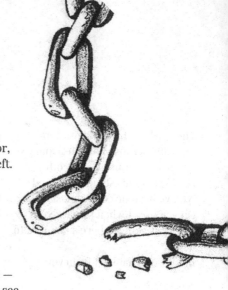

Creeping over creaking floorboard,
Clothes over the long of my shoulder,
I edge closer - when the click of a door,
A holler, a breathe, and a motor — I left.
Hurling over the broad of his porch,
Sprinting half naked through a jungle
Of dimly lit caravans with no torch.

Lead by the ferocity of a lust for life
I ran faster than men before me
With pain, sweat, semen, blood, strife —
With paths dark, but sweet enough to see.
Over the road, behind the alley of a shop,
For the first time in months I feel
breathe,
From lungs anew pumping non-stop,
I vomit over a notice, crying, so to heave
Freedom.

He will be looking for me in his car,
He knows where I live, and where I sleep,
Wherever I run, he'll not be too far,
But now I'm not so scared of that freak.
So for four hours, I scoped the back
lanes,
Finding my way home in the wee hours,
And my body expelled most of the pain,
And I fainted upon the Amaryllis flowers.

libre por fin

And so,
with no sun, or water,
or love, alone —
the dragonsnap dies.

My Garden

When I cast an eye over my garden,
my heart pardons
Everything;
For it is so beautiful.
Here grows the hearts and minds of
the bad times
And the good,
Evolving and solving
Upon little green stems,
Healing and kneeling before a sun
So remarkably unforgiving,
Yet so very beautiful,
So very necessary
For both growth and survival
Of the leaves and beaming blooms:
The raucous rays of reverence
Give their best to test the flowers
As they learn to show.
O, as an eye hovers
Over my colours
They know I am a survivor,
Nay a sufferer!
As aromas hijack the senses
No one will jump these fences
Again as they've become stronger
Just like their gardener.
You don't need gloves to know
The beds are flooded with love,
Hardship.
As they stand the winter months,
My garden shows triumph
Hazing out, hazing in:

The cold can no longer hurt me.

DAEDALIAN

When he weeps inwardly
To conceal his mad misery
And fickle iniquity
Know that it's because of you
—

you are the nothing.

My tears are the fruit of my body,
and the salt of my soul.

Lune d'Avril

Underneath the April moon
We lay embraced until noon
And hummed tipsy tunes

In each-others doting glow
We talked
Of tomorrow and next year,
Together we'd face no fear,
Clutching hands through tears,

But oh,
How the sky mimicked Mars,
Whipping trickles of red stars,
A voyeur to this new found love of ours,

I will love you
Until the stars dampen

The Lively Loom

The coltish carry on in the coming
of a new day,
The demurred kisses beset with
our eyes shut tight,
For we need not know each-other
as we steal way,
Under the warm allure of love's
amorous bite.

As dawning daybreak finally broke
open our eyes,
We caught ourselves reticent while
getting dressed,
Then I walked you to the bus when
under fair skies,
You kissed me unapologetically
and I knew I was blessed.

And now, three score and ten,
she's no longer with me,
And I sit alone at dinner rejoicing
with old thought,
Her kiss, her heart and glance are
burned into memory,
And that afternoon glance I have
never, ever forgot.

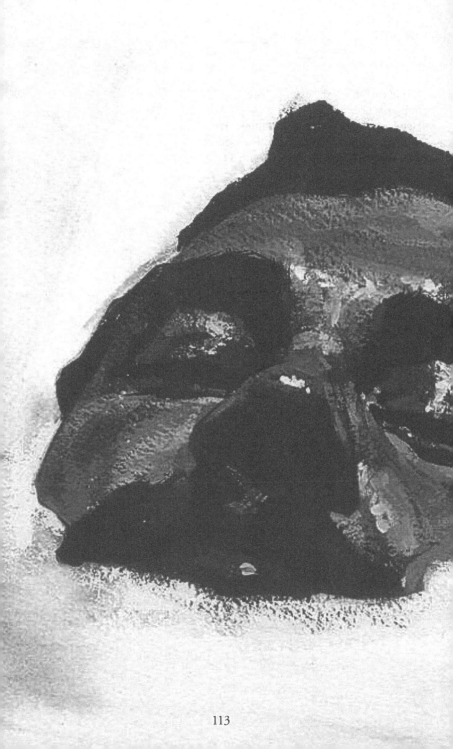

Catalina

It is of earthiness she exumes true
quintessence,
Her eyes exudes complete beguiling grace,
With an aura extravasating gentle essence,
Two emerald pools impressed upon a face.

A lustrous epidermis of porcelain
impeccability,
Her hair a shadow from the blackened sun,
A jaw contoured from the might of
delectability,
A heart beating like a tribal drum.

In the world's field of strive she is courage,
In the se faire du souci of life she is
refinement,
She embellishes authenticity in her visage
absolute,
Even in the midst of imperative
confinement.

Her name is consummate,
Her name is idyllic,
Her name is —
Catalina.

Ne Plus Ultra

The Nymphaea nelumbo flower
isn't reluctant of abundant growth,
With superlative simpatico and
bona fides Brobdingnagian,
She effortlessly masters both.

Gracious gazes convoy with her
winsome episodes of doubtful dazes,
The jocular altruistic candour met
with mirthful magnanimity,
She tries and she amazes.

Heart rending poignance translates
her homely capacity and substance,
Femininity challenged and
championed to galvanise,
Every heartbeat is a dance.

Ad finem, the paragons embodies
the flower's fluency fraught
with the finesse it is fortified with,
She knows it not,
But she is the ne plus ultra.

kåt räv

She dreams of millionaires,
but received a Machiavellian
boy,
He would lay her down on
weekdays and perk her up on
weekends,
Never so invigorating is the
rigid end of warm teeth on
the end of such soft nipples,
Rivers ran even when they
held hands,
One a plant with a seed,
The other a hand filled.The
tender kisses on the eyelids
of beauty was commonplace,
but the river never dried up,
Even in the summer she the
temperatures soared,
A relationship built on
mischievous sex neither to
harm nor to hurt,
But to excite,
Legs that climb the whole
way up,
Breasts that invite dark eyes
to their touch,
A body that could make the
angels mourn,

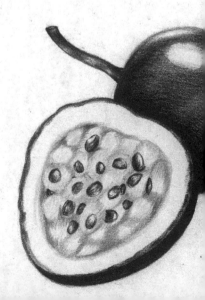

At night in bed before I sleep
She sharpies penises on my forehead
And I've never felt love like this before.

Panes

It's perplexing.
He, so cruel.
His eyes are glazed
over.
No one behind them.
Only you in them.
You breathing for him,
Causing vaporous fog
in his head,
Hurting, hideously
inclined,
Skin shedding sweat,
sour odours.
There's someone in
that head,
Behind the glass,
Scraping panes,
Screeching,
Trying to break —
His gaze.

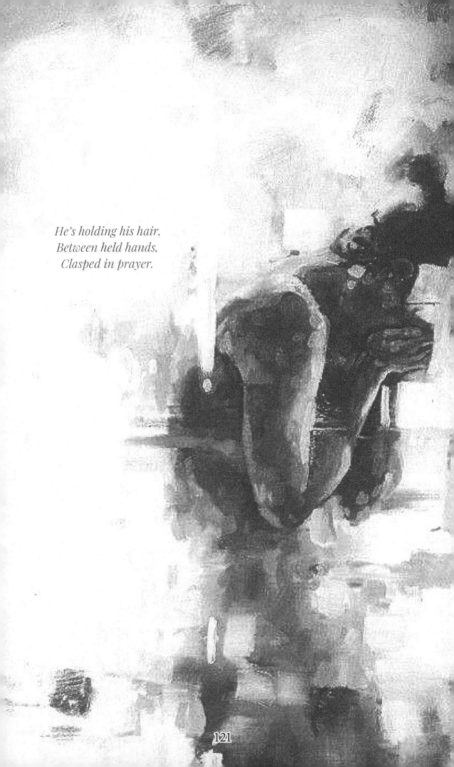

He's holding his hair,
Between held hands,
Clasped in prayer.

Paper

I can't hear you cry
anymore at night.
When you scream, you
don't need me.
Why do you stick around?
For the impossible.
I can see friends standing
over you.
They're flickering as flame
does.
But you cannot see it.
And they will keep you
warm in the dark.
Always an arms reach.
Let your heart heft into
their hot hands.
Hook their arms so that
they may share the weight.
For they flicker like flames.
Let the pain sink away
beneath your feet and into
the earth.
And feel it grow into fruit
which can be eaten.

Act like you feel
And you won't won't hear
the sound
Of me getting older
And my heart moulder,

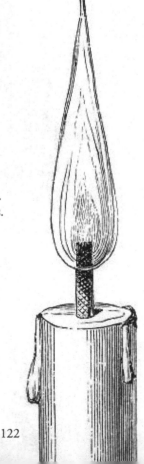

Truest

I don't know how,
I wouldn't know where to begin,
And you wouldn't want to listen if I
began to ramble.
Do you really want to hear me
ramble?
Tell me you don't.
You and I;
A faux pas.

I cannot bring myself to tell you
who I am,
Because as merciful as you are,
You'd abandon me,
Because it's what I truly deserve.
I'd beg,
I'd steal,
And I'd borrow,
For you just to understand that
I'm not well.

I did it to keep you
interested,
Not to deceive you,
Unmindful of the mountain I
was building,
Do you still love me?
Tell me you still love me...
Don't you?

I didn't mean to steal
years away,
I just wanted children
with you,
And a happy life,
Unaware of my blunders,
I just want love.
Validation.

Fold this little edge,
Cut across the page,
Step onto the ledge,
And leave the rest to rage.

When we are stuck with it.
We moan together.
Why we groan atonally
Who knows?
Where it takes us is a secret but
watch what happens

      when it grows...

Duffle

This is us, eh?
Nothing to say,
Take a coat
Be on your way,
And as it darkens,
That's another day,
For you and me.

I sell you,
I sell you,
We sell all of
We sell all of our life.

We once carried
Firm shoulders,
And now we bare
Weary efforts,
For you and me,

But what occurs,
Whatever jars,
Is all that's left,
Need we want more?

Take your coat,
No, take my coat,
Mine'll keep you warm,
Yours will just hurt.

I want you to say you love me,
For no cost,
Just because you do so,
And keep me warm,
Come, keep me warm,
Is your heart torn?

00:07

Seven minutes past midnight
And somewhere between the pillow
And the ceiling
There is a mind screaming for love.

He often cries there pondering,
'What does he have that I do not?'
So he opened his browning heart
And began to make a start.

'Is he bigger than me,' he yelled at walls,
'Can he kiss your lips more tender?'
This lust had endured long delusion
For her lips he could not remember.

He made his bed and over-read
The off thoughts in his head,
While pocketing his wary hands
As cramps beset his forehead.

'When did she stop?' he wondered,
'Was she looking for something in return?'
But he knew even if he demanded her faith
He was aware he'd still never learn.

'You don't deserve me,' he declared,
'I detest your denial of my love so
I'll never let you love again,
And I'll never let you go.'

How low he sank into his bedclothes that night
Her eyes the seed of his stubborn badness,
He tussled around with her in his pillow
For now he knew nothing but sadness,

Frank

Noble soul, do not love me,
Love the one who keeps you warm;
Sing for him in his sleep,
For my love for you has worn.

It's been too long since we kissed
On the banks near the river's bed,
And even though you are truly missed,
My love for you is dead.

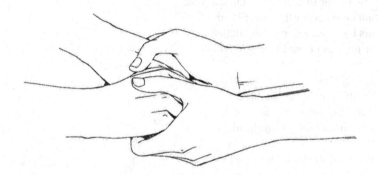

The Bridge

It's okay I'll just turn up my music and
look away,
And I'll let you go on your way,
Every second we walk nearer to one
another,
In the corner of my eyes
I am recognised,
By your adoring mother,
And my little crestfallen heart dies,
While in tandem we ignore eachother.

And so we pass.

Seconds later I can hear you over the
song,
Telling your mum what went wrong,
While stones bounce around my
fluttering gut,
With my eyes so inflamed,
I am ashamed,
That our ties are now cut,
With my pride so soundly maimed,
And from their hearts I am now shut.

And so we part.

Tomorrow I won't be waking up in
your bed,
And I'll get that into my head,
Though a sofa isn't the most
comfortable rest,
It's what I deserve,
For I'm unlearned,
With you were my principal arrest,
And for me you cannot be earned,
For I am not willing to give my best.

And the bridge burns.

Many-hued upon introduction,
Both begrimed by the ending,
There are times when she dawns his
thoughts and in turn his self destruction,
He wastes too much time spending,

471 days have passed since civil breath was
broken and many moons since the two
paramours have spoken,
He likes to like thinking about thinking too
much for such is the psyche he dug for
himself and the way of life he chose.

Insecurities seized the heart before an entente
was settled with his hubris,
Once amiable eyes filled with her now absent
culpable bowls of woe,
Posture and lip pursing pride to hopelessly
hide his bruises.

To his chagrin the spirit is crushed by her
inamorato in a bout of doltish cacoethes,
Sequestered to the unplumbed depths of
melancholia his heart churns his ardour,
Festered proposals to conclude the mortal
game ensue with the use of little keys.

Solitary sublimity ignited his vital need to
be heard for he grew sheepish of words,
He matured in the shadow of his ghost
becoming host to a more forthright being;
Seeing how alarmingly the mind blossomed
unyielding as though he had taken flight
with the birds.

471 days later, and he became sad he would
cry: Despondency is merely a feather in the
cap of faculty,
And releasing the fit of pique finally taught
him how to fly.

But just when he let go,
He missed the pain of hanging on,
And his hands began to glow,
For a heart he held onto for so long.

panacea

Mother, when you asked me why I
hadn't chosen a lover while the
belfry's screamed
I told you my heart isn't one to be
sold for it's far too extreme,
Though you did ask again I
pretended not to hear,
For fear that I would fall to my knees
and erupt into tears.

Mother, know that I choose to walk
alone to heal myself and not to
brutally hurt you,
I decide to be alone because in the
bowels of my soul I deserve it so very
true,
Lovers still line up in modest
numbers for I attracted the
nonpareil,
But alas, their decent frames and
warm gestures are to no avail.

I choose not to swallow poison for
you because you beg to know what
and who I am,
I am your son, bolstering a tungsten
heart which belongs to none, woman
or man,
However, in your mind I am nothing
more than bewildered and detached,
And you fail to grasp that loneliness
isn't a curse - it's medicine
unmatched.

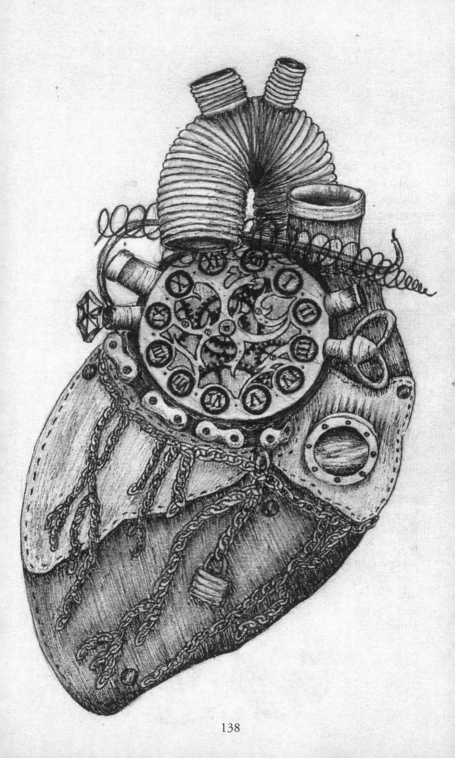

Amici

Maybe it's just the Sambucca talking,
But when you're over here rocking
At my chest with a heart knocking,
Tomorrow, you'll find it difficult walking
Out my door with hips, still so supple, sore.

You're just as much a whore as I am
A lamb following you wherever you land,
Or lay, and I'm not ashamed of who I am,
Entirely, but know I haven't touched a gram
Since your brother, Sam, frittered that grand.

Who the fuck do we think we really are?
Short of strength, consistency, will-power
To keep our eyes, our hands, our hearts
Our lips from the heat of one-another
For less than forty-eight empty, torturous hours.

I see you and Jack on through the smoke
Of booths, holding something rather broke
Between the whiskey and coke; not a joke
Passed between friendly faces on coke
Or the idiotic rumble of his father-bought yolk,
soaked.

I know he hits you, every one of us do,
But with that make-up how can we prove
It, how can we justify giving him bruises —
Letting him know he has someone to lose?
I'm not perfect, but this won't be the life you
choose?

Just like last night, just come on with me
To my flat near Cappagh, and you can feel
My love again, or come camp under trees
Near the railways to feel that nippy breeze
On our arses through things no one will believe.

Or stay there in his those arms till you cry,
Until Annie comes with palms to wipe dry
Your tears in that smoking area beside
Parked police cars — or come let me drive
You back to where we used to touch, used to
survive.

Little blue lines,
Tell me it's true.
Tell me it's mine,
Part fear into my hands
With courage in her heart
To make a decision.

Dadaí

I see you hiding behind street corners,
and I know you —
that face.
I've seen those lines before.
When I gave a goodbye in Larne you
knelt behind my dustbins.
I just let you watch me cry, without
saying a word.
When I boarded on the coast I heard
you in my the water pipes.
Why couldn't you just knock the door?
Still, I kissed you goodnight.
I remember you sitting beside me
when I was giving birth.
But you were hidden behind an old
newspaper.
I couldn't quite catch you when you
caught that tram —
Though, I'll know I'll see you soon.
I'll leave my windows open, my doors
ajar, my mind wavering.
I need to see that face again, to feel it's
lines.
There's my little face in those
brows.Have we hidden before?
Omagh, 1998, I saw you laughing.
With a face red with joy.
Gone in a quick-flick second.
You looked so incredibly happy.
A piece of you still lies with me, held
with small hands on a choked chest.
You looked so very bright.
You looked so very blurry.
When I sleep that's all I see with loud
noises scuffling and screaming.
And when my dusty eyes open I see
you —But you're not quite there.

The Melody Of Molly Patterson

The melody of Molly,
The melody of folly
To all those who
Meet her eyes
And feel her whole heart,
For it plays so smoothly,
Here it says;

'Molly Patterson loves to love,
And everyone loves to love her,
For every kiss is from above,
Every kiss is a stir.'

She chooses him wisely,
Seeking organic courtesy.
Chauvinists she has surpassed,
With their impartial audacity.
To those who shun she sings
The melody of Molly:

'Our Molly is never ashamed,
Of who she is, or who she sees,
Her sweet song can quench rains,
Echoing through the breeze.'

She is the peony of Polerone,
She is the rose of Rathdrum,
She is the sunflower of Swords,
And she'll float past on a cloud.

'For she is Molly Patterson,
With adoration off the chart.
For she loves to have fun,
Boasting a big heart.'

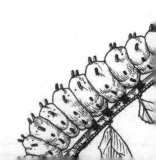

Six Little Days

My eyes just won't open,
My lips just won't stop moving,
And I want to dream,
But even in there it crawls over us.
I need help.
What are we supposed to do?
Hang low till it blows over?
Cover our ears until they stop?
He says work has him stressed,
She said wasn't impressed,
Happiness comes to a halt,
He says she made him do it,
She said it's all his fault.
And we're left here in the corner,
Crossing our heads like a tennis match,
Eyes eating the words,
And ears opening to the odds.
She'll leave to learn,
Give it six days then return,
He'll take a joint,
Then leave just to prove some point,
Though we'll still be here,
Starving and stamping our little feet,
Hoping someone will give something,
But when warned man and wife quarrel —
There is no sense, no time, no feeling.

Don't fuss, I'll just get a taxi.
No need to do everything for me.
I knew this wouldn't be very easy.
Go and make yourself some tea.
And take care of yourself.

I left my key in your pocket,
Saving the door from being knocked,
If only I was as clear as I talked,
My mind wouldn't be as rocked —
But I'm not good at it.

Chair's Edge

I've never touched that coat again,
Because you're buried in those pockets,
I shan't cry, or even try to pretend,
For now, I'll attempt to forget
You were even here in these arms,
In these memories and moments,
Held together with choppy charms,
And a child — from god she was sent.

You went too far on this time over,
But I knew it was over long before,
Long before we found any closure,
Long before you unlocked the door,
Just before we embraced on New Years,
Through a fear we wouldn't survive,
Scarring her through her teenage years,
And the chance of a life we'd derive.

She often asks where you've gone,
And I smile and I hold her and I say;
'Don't worry, Molly, she won't be long,
She might come back, just not today.'
To which she doesn't really respond,
More-so reluctantly continues to play,
Play beside the door looking beyond,
Over the hillsides, searching for mummy.

You've ignored all of my phone calls
You're ignoring all of my text messages,
And she doesn't deserve this at all,
Please don't send her to an orphanage.
I'll put it down if you come on back home,
Because I can't do this all on my own,
Come on back before you're unknown,
Come on back before she's grown.

Or don't — and watch her grow short,
Grow short of a mother's towering touch,
And a life seldom lived outside of court,
Weeping why she never asked for much.
You can sit wherever you are in silence,
Letting her dance her way into sadness,
Knowing you can do something of substance,
Knowing you ignore her out of gladness.

So at a chairs edge I desperately beg,
Come home, come and love her, not I,
For my entire life I have sullied with mistake,
Misfortune, depression, feeling and lies.
Do it for the star who reaches on out,
To eyes so milky, yet so dark and alone,
Let her know what true-love is all about,
So please, love, for Molly — come on home.

CATATONIA 2

Ten, she can't pretend
Nine, she's behind time
Eight, it could be too late
Seven, time to touch heaven
Six, fatigued in a fix
Five, too large to stay alive
Four, too big to ignore
Three, so little to feel,
Two, nothing to lose,
One, up, up in the sun

Lift off.

Dust

Keep an eye on the horizon, for
she grows colder,
Remembering her niece and son,
looking over her shoulder,
And be wary as you watch her, for
she'll duck down,
Steady-on skyward, copy that,
Roger, over and out.

Blue burns out into black, where
metal smells charred,
With an astronautical attack, for
alone is her heart,
Deprived of gallant tact, sunk
down in glassy parts,
What button did she touch?
Did they give her far too much?
Still she ascends.

What's with those eyes?
Are you looking for threats?
Millions of little green cries,
Underneath her helmet,
Caught in the curling controls,
Pinching in little places,
And it never stops being cold,
While she peeps out into space.

Mission control, do you read me
Mission control?
There's footprints beyond the
Flagpole,
And her Stars and Stripes are lost.

Terror

The Leonids leap into her launch pads
Directing debris to dwindle in an steel-clad
Ensemble encircling an empty comrade
Before a shuttle rocked around a triad
Of immense meteorite, moulding her GAD
Through time in this clapping of a hand,
Expanding over the having and the had;
Almost sad the bad will soon turn mad.

There's a simple supermassive mess
Over shoulders buckling with duress
Under zero-gravity's travelling test
With arms folded over a failing chest
Somewhere between the worst, the best
Years of a life lived always near a nest
Crumbling with her loved-ones abreast—
The melting sunlight putting echos to rest.

She's floating past infinity with an
asteroid,
Signals silenced and dead,
Clinging onto a space capsule with the
orbiters destroyed,
She will never return home.

She will turn a star or two and she'll
make no friends,
No noise,
In her throat or in her head with
Luna's sweet lunacy,
Rolling around the rays of infrared.

The world wallows away in the
distance,
Waving like an endearing aunt,
Blowing kisses to meaningless
existence,
She wishes to go home but she can't.

It's another level of loneliness
And the silence is so deafening,
With hard human lowliness
Reaching up for a reckoning,
The most exquisite isolation
Yet nothing to comfort and hold
Except endless meditation
Amidst the consuming cold.

Too young to die...
Yet too old to care
For she has lived life
And seen it's snare.

Raving

Now she's dancing with death in a
manner unexpected,
Waltzing down the aisle of darkness,
Drinking in the voices of ones she
once protected,
She feels too scared to confess,
Secrets she sours at even space
growing to know,
Not that it'll mean anything of matter,
But it might take the glimmer out of
Earth's glow,
So she withholds the clatter,

Now she suspects she's survived the
first day,
Breathing in the little she has,
Crying because there's a closeted care
to convey,
But there's a time to pass,

Hung up hot on the love for low solid
land,
She forgets her feet, her arms, her
hands,
She forgets what her family, her
friends,
But does she forget her own face?
Well that depends.

She won't get down,
And it gets her down

Visible Light

My lungs are filled With a breath and a body
Lying in the garden
When blood busts to bruise
The hems of the heart
Beyond the lonely licked liver
Tucked in tickles of fat
Adjuring the ask of an interlude
For it's slowly giving way
And we all know I can't just keep my giggles aside
So we'll deal with it another day.

The solidity of sentimentality
Dissolves down in a tumbler
Yet the pain still prays without gravity
You're trapped, now get out
Touching the trembling figures afar
More muffled than a muttering
Though behind their babbling teeth
Someone's saving your sickly skin.

But you flaff them away, like flies,
Throwing them out like old magazines
For you want hardships to get harder
Because it confirms a cup overfloweth
Peaks a pitiful prize, while portraits pitter,
You slur yourself to wonder, 'does any of it matter?'

We feel you peeling, like old wallpaper,
Don't let go of yourself in the drapes,
Don't let go of yourself as you caper,
Very soon you'll be on the roof
Or dancing down a dawn
For there's nothing needed anymore
Nothing wanted, it's between your fingers
Swirling in the dim dinging room
Swinging in a shallow seated tomb
And one day we'll be back
To ask what we could've done.

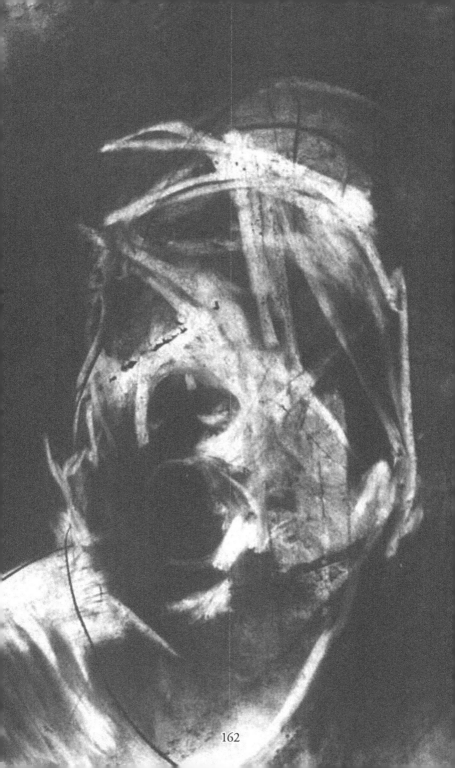

Hand-Held

Beneath a corkscrew and the tearing labels,
she nosedives willingly
For there are things she wants to destroy
Tear limb from limb, and cast into the drains
street-side,
And all the pipes, the rivers will bring them
back
And she'll pour one more
Till she breaks the door.

She frequently falls from Neptune on a knock
And only then would she talk
Of the heartaches she endured
With black holes all hand-held
On the crust of the mighty moon-bed
Her worries down below.

What is she supposed to do?
The signals just gone dead, there no sign of
her crew,
The compass can choose
Where she ends up next and how she empties
her blues
What am she supposed to do?
It's all so hopeless, so that's nothing totally
new.

Through the blue and the grey,
Waits another little day
Through the shroud and the cloud,
Lies mayhem aloud,
Through the madness of that place,
She might be better off in space.

Older Than Time

Set my scene,
On tiles we're yet to clean,
Glimmering above,
Before I've had quite enough.

My daughters,
Raised, like lambs to slaughter,
My only son,
His pain has only just begun.

While men camp out far
Between night and day, I will remember
Twisting thorns in my side
And I won't allow it to die.

I won't let things go
Manifesting until they grow
Like bitching buzzards on badgers
Crumbling quick as cadavers
For I refuse to pay the Titan's toll
For if needs be I shall grow cold
For I'm off, and effort is too old
So I take with teeth all I can hold.

My sisters,
Burning me back like blisters
Binning the lids?
So they took my kids.

Now the house sleeps
Inside, where cries keep,
And how is this living
When I don't feel like giving?

My mind is a blockhouse
Observing the kippers and she-clowns
Twisting thorns in my side,
And I won't allow it to die.

That Little Something

More than food she wants time,
She yearns to know the time,
For ultimately she is timeless
And epochs belong to nihility,
More than food she wants water,
Adam's ale, off a helmet screen,
Licking the seeping mists,
Blinking to stay awake.

How long have I been here
Everything looks the same
Every star, every planet, is just a scarring
reminder
That she thinks she's innately insane
Loosing the lost, loving the lights.

She swears she can see birds
Buzzing by Betelgeuse,
Shedding feathers over forbidden lines and
flare stars,
She swears she can hear noise,
Voices voluminous over Venus,
Raining down onto acid clouds with words so
sultry.

Even in space she's an outsider,
Feeling really regrettable,
With no curtains to hide her,
Tricky, lost, and forgettable.

Battling with Orion's Belt,
While the earth sleeps,
Rolling, bowling out of control,
Trying to earn her keep.

Even the stars won't shine on her,
Keeping her colder,
So she'll freeze out into the void,
Vacuum at the ready,
Humming little frequencies,
Heaven and hell, pushing and pulling.

Saiph For Now

Safe under swabs of Saiph's luminous kiss,
Aching stiff; slowly fading,
Blood in the mouth of an underbelly of piss,
Lonesome, nothing's degrading.

And she can smell herself scared,
The final scents the universe shared,
Whispering she must be prepared,
To bid ta-ra to his chef-d'œuvre,
To bid ta-ra to the masterworks.

Santa Muerte scuffles up a ring
And bends into empty ears to sing
Words of the unknown, and the lost,
Where side-ways she'd plunge into chaos,
So the screens came up.

And we were down here looking up,
Seeing you move across the moon,
And mum; I think we always knew,
You'd never come back down
Unless it was in flames,
Devastating planes as you
Pretend to know our names,
Wanting the fantasy.

We'd often sigh aloud together
While bottles roll around the moon

Vacuums

I can't imagine
What it's like to feel nothing in space,
I can't imagine the cold,
Though I can never stop crying,
neither can you,
Four fingers covering a face,
And we both know why we weep.

We eagerly await the day
When you fall out of that sky
Down onto the hard horizon
Breathing, hoping, determined to die.

I hope your hiding from us,
Because we know you need some
space right now,
You come back when you want,
We will be waiting, arms open,
We'll be ready to catch you, snatch
you from harm,
Just take little breaths.

We know you hide them,
Under beds, behind the wardrobes,
For you need to know, so we don't,
And you've failed,
Those are the waters ripping us apart,
Choices and well known voices will
get you started.

The sick's off your pillows,
The shopping's been done,
Dad won't stop looking to the sun,
He's hurting, but it never shows,
He shelters here on Earth,
Because even though you don't get
on, he loves you,
He'll help you back down.

When you come back,
Neve and Ana need some time,
For they don't understand pain yet,
But hold onto them like air,
Surely, steadily they'll return,
You know how girls are.

Please tell me you'll be back soon,
Because the house is so quiet,
Aunt Lucia doesn't rise till noon,
And the rest tend to riot.

Know through the tears
And through the flares,
That we're all still here,
And we all still care.

Please, mam.
Come back to Earth.

Crying In The Cosmos

Shake those shackles off,
Short and sewn inside,
Scars make you tough,
Then their heads collide,
And weins reluctantly descry
The jingly shackles shaking
Bleaching babes brains
Making everything seem normal,
But she needs help into bed,
Before she hurt her head anymore,
She's not making sense, but pain does that,
She's hard on the defence, but pain does that.
Who's ever truly fine?
Who's nothing on their mind?
There's always something,
There's always that someone
So why is there nothing?
Let them out into cupped hands, then put it out,
Meeting the night like cigarette ash,
You're on the news, in my dreams,
They say you're definitely deceased,
But I hear that heart, it's singing,
Sealed away in a tarry chest locked before May.

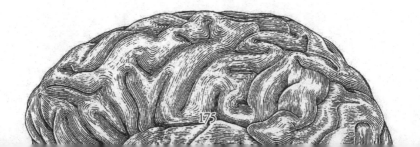

Spitting up smoke,
Spitting up ashtrays,
But you're not beaten so,
There's piff in these engines,
Heating up to take you on home,
Ignition, into the third dimension,
Wake up in there,
Don't choke on the hurt, breathe,
Awake before teatime,
Don't eat the walls of your mouth,
Vomit, blood, both problematic,
Sink the sun, eat the nebula,
Feel the cold, it'll bring you back to us,
Feel the cold, it'll save you from yourself,
More shackles than keys,
Leant on stomaches,
What a shame,Will she get back?
Will she cut us some slack?
Will she be the same?
How meek is she?
Enough to be herself?
Bring me the book on that shelf,
And read her back to health,
Forget about yourself,
Forget about those men,
Think of someone else.

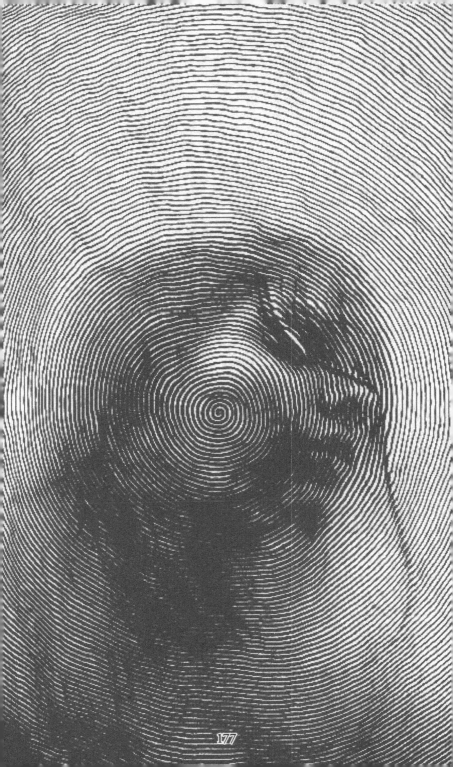

Solway

Kiss those cheeks.
Cut that hair.
Give me a little smile,
But don't stare.
And don't speak.
Your feet are filthy, but onward
you leap.
The sun consoles,
Where a wind whips cold.
It's in your eyes.
Dirt and dust gets stuck in your
sighs,
Coughing it up as you loudly laugh.
I see your messily combed hair, but
I won't stare.
I stand behind you.
So near you all.
I feel tears through plastic,
Crying, unbeknownst.
Unable to communicate.
Your blouse is full of bluebirds.
Beautiful bluebirds, alone in the
nest,
No mother to help and to hold
them,
Off somewhere in a universe
untold with duelling stars and
spaceships.
You're happier, wholesome
without me and I understand.

What kind of love is this?
The kind without a kiss.
With a heart sorely missed,
I'll wave just wave over the way
And smile behind screens.
I love you so much.
I feel my palms pulsing through
gloves.
Tensing, twitching, sweating.
In the crash of a flash,
I can't find you anymore.
The fields are bare
And empty.
Left are bits of blouse, beautiful
bluebirds chirping cheerfully,
Without a mother to help and
hold them.
She's gone - Lucia.
I've seldom been satisfied.
Pride more powerful than love,
As you fly in skies I spied,
Swooping low, soaring high.
If I'm still out there,
I'll be fine.
I'll be survive.

Friendly Faces

It might take me back
To the timber table
To the timely tribulation
The woman within me
Is opening her eyes to faces
Friendly in my bed, reading to me,
Combing my hair, bringing me tea,
Standing with lanterns,
Faces in red hands raw.
So much emotion
Between mirrors and my mouth,
I feel it on the air.
I feel guilty but greater
For being given a chance.
But it's dangerous
To rest on wild words, thirsty thoughts,
Primed promises, and drying roses.
But I can't let them down,
Because they brought me back
To a world full of hate, and of hope,
Full of life and laughter,
Flowing with fire and smoke.
I'll taste a song so sweet,
And wait long if needs be.
What I have is more than enough,
Grateful for it's grace,
For if this place truly is hell;
It's definitely better than space.

Printed in the United States
By Bookmasters